Living Single

30 Devotionals for Women Who Love God and Want a Husband

Lisa K. Satchell

Cover design by Nicholas Davison

Editorial services by Morgan E. Ball

ISBN-13: 979-8-7047-2149-9

Dedicated to God:
for showing me how to love myself, others, and my future
husband.

Contents

30 Devotionals for Women Who Love God
and Want a Husband

A Letter for You

Hey Girl!

I hope you're doing well. To say I'm excited to have you read this book is an understatement. I'm getting a little ahead of myself, though. My name is Lisa K. Satchell, and from this point on we're no longer strangers - we're sisters. So, if I call you "Sis," don't be surprised.

A little about me - I've never been in a relationship. I promise you, it is not for lack of trying or wanting. It is fully a part of God's will for my life. While I love following His path and His path only, there have been some tough moments of self-doubt, impatience, and frustration. But God, being the loving Father that He is, has comforted me and given me revelation through it all. This book is a collection of those revelations that I had to share with you.

So, a head's up about what you're going to encounter with this book - each devotional includes a Scripture, some thoughts I wanted to share with you, a prayer, and a journal prompt. In case you see a Bible translation you're not familiar with, I've included a key in the back of the book. I highly encourage you to interact with this book in a quiet space. It can be when you first wake up, when you're preparing to go to bed, or during a small moment of peace that you may acquire throughout your day. Be sure to allow yourself time and space to feel and digest everything that you read.

I pray that this book blesses you and reminds you of who you are in Christ Jesus.

Love you, Sis!

How Do You Feel?

Psalms 139:17-18 TPT
"Every single moment you are thinking of me! How precious and wonderful to consider that you cherish me constantly in your every thought! O God, your desires toward me are more than the grains of sand on every shore! When I awake each morning, you're still with me."

Okay - so before we really get into this, you need to take a moment and identify how you really feel about being single. Are you sick of not having a man? Do you love the freedom of being single? Do you wish you could cuddle with someone? Do you enjoy your personal space? Are you a mix of all of these emotions and more?

I ask these questions because it's important that we be honest with ourselves and God. God is all-knowing. He knows how we feel better than we do. However, being transparent with Him helps us to build a relationship with Him. Before and after we get married, our relationship with God should be the most important thing to us. He already has a crazy amount of love for us. Building our relationship with Him to be even stronger through our transparency is a win-win situation.

Prayer

God, I thank You that You know me so intimately. I pray that You would help me to be transparent with You about my feelings of singleness. I know that no matter what I'm feeling, You will be in it with me, giving me joy and peace. In Jesus' name, amen!

Journal

Take a moment and journal about how you feel in your singleness. Be as honest and transparent as you can. Once you're done, have a talk with God and share your feelings with Him.

_____

_____

_____

_____

_____

_____

_____

_____

_____

_____

Let Go & Let God

Jeremiah 29:11-12 NLT
"For I know the plans I have for you," says the Lord. "They are plans for good and not for disaster, to give you a future and a hope. In those days when you pray, I will listen."

As much as this may be annoying to hear, your relationship with your future husband is something you have no real control over. Your man is a whole other human with his own thoughts, feelings, and ideals. You can't truly make him date you, fall in love with you, or even be the person you think he can be. That's 100% all in God's hands. There will be moments when we'll want to help God. We may try to make the first move with a man, knowing good and well God didn't lead us to do that. We may even start dating someone just based on potential and try to fix them through our relationship with them. Actions like these that are not God-led can leave us hurt, frustrated, and brokenhearted.

So with that in mind, what should we do? We're out here single like a dollar bill. At this point, the best thing we can do is pray. Release everything to God. Is there a man you want that isn't acting right? Ask God to remove the desire for that man from your heart if he isn't the one. If you're feeling bold, you can even ask God to reveal why he's acting up. Your specific situation may not be listed here, but I'm sure there's a situation or experience in your life - romantically or otherwise - where you could give full control to God. He is all-knowing and powerful. He can cause anything to happen. Let Him take it on.

Prayer
God, I give You full control over my love life and relationships. I pray that You would remove from me any urge to take things on without Your guidance or assistance. I thank You that You love me and only want what's best for me. I pray for Your good and perfect will over my life. In Jesus' name, amen!

Journal
Write down an area of your life where you need to give God full control. Think of something that is completely out of your hands with no way for you to act on it. Write out the reasons you may be struggling to give God control. When you're done, pray over it and allow God to take it out of your hands.

_____

_____

_____

_____

_____

_____

_____

_____

_____

_____

_____

_____

_____

_____

_____

Be Patient & Hopeful

Romans 12:12 TPT
"Let this hope burst forth within you, releasing a continual joy. Don't give up in a time of trouble, but commune with God at all times."

I know we've all heard the saying, "Patience is a virtue." Though it can be a cliché, it's very true. Patience is an admirable quality that we should all strive to possess. However, there are a bunch of other emotions and thoughts that get in the way of our patience. In my personal situation, I know God has a husband for me. I trust and know that when the time is right, God will bring us together. With that being said, I do have moments where I'm like, "God, where is my man? Why isn't he here yet? Your girl has been single too long." Then I remember that relationships take two to tango.

When we go through moments of being frustrated that God hasn't brought us our men yet, we have to remember that there are two lives He's working in. Maybe our future husbands are going through something that requires them to be single at the moment. Maybe there are still some areas of growth that we could develop in before God brings us our men. Because we're only human, we can't see everything going on. We're working with limited information, but thankfully we have God who knows all. He is molding us and our husbands into great matches for each other. God is aware that you've been patient. When the time is right, you and your man will spend years together creating memories and making up for any time you feel like you may have lost.

Prayer

God, I thank You for working on the behalf of me and my future husband. Even when we have moments of being impatient with Your timing, You remain patient with us. I pray that You would soften my heart and build up my patience. I wait with expectancy that You are going to do amazing things as a result of my patience. In Jesus' name, amen!

Journal

Take a moment and write down some things that excite you about having a relationship. When you're done writing, tell God what you're excited for.

_____

_____

_____

_____

_____

_____

_____

_____

_____

_____

_____

_____

_____

_____

_____

_____

_____

_____

_____

_____

_____

_____

_____

_____

_____

_____

Do it Now!

Ecclesiastes 9:7 NLT
"So go ahead. Eat your food with joy, and drink your wine with a happy heart, for God approves of this!"

Have you ever thought, "Once I get my man I'll ____?" This 'blank' could be about traveling, going to a restaurant you've always wanted to go to, or anything else you might be waiting to do. If we think about it for real, is there a reason we have to be in a relationship to do these things? There are some trips or activities we could do now with our friends or even just by ourselves with God.

Sometimes we can act like our lives are on hold until we meet our man. Though our husbands will be a great addition to our lives, they'll be just that - additions. If you want to travel, your man will definitely be a great travel buddy. However, that doesn't mean you have to wait for him to start planning a trip. If you want to try a fancy restaurant, you can get a group of your friends together and have a girls' night. When you all get your men, they'll be great additions for a group date. Even if you just want someone to relax with and watch a movie, you can invite God to join you for some one-on-one time. When you get your man, all three of y'all can enjoy a movie night. Basically, what I'm saying is that we can do it all NOW. There's no reason to put our lives on hold just because we're single.

Prayer
God, thank You for another day to live my life and do what I love. I pray that You would allow me to be open-minded to new experiences and new opportunities to have fun. I pray that You would be with me as I experience new things and set out on adventures. In Jesus' name, amen!

Journal
What are some things you may be putting off for when you get your man? Write them out and see if you can do them sooner rather than later. Truly consider opening up the experience to friends, family, or even just a solo adventure with God.

_____

_____

_____

_____

_____

_____

_____

_____

_____

_____

_____

_____

_____

_____

_____

_____

_____

_____

_____

_____

_____

_____

_____

_____

_____

_____

_____

You Don't Have to Change

Psalm 139: 13-14 NKJV
"For You formed my inward parts; You covered me in my mother's womb. I will praise You, for I am fearfully and wonderfully made; Marvelous are Your works, And that my soul knows very well."

Have you ever thought, "I need to ___ so my man will come?" Whether that blank has to do with losing weight, making a certain amount of money, or achieving a goal, statements and thoughts like these place unfair expectations on us. I promise you, the man God has for you will love you no matter what you weigh, how much money you have, or what goals you have accomplished. You know how I know? Because God loves you regardless of all of that! He thinks you're beautiful, successful, smart, and kind just the way you are. And because God loves you for you, He's more than capable of sending you a man who will love you for you.

I say all of this to say, if there are things in your life you feel like you want to accomplish, be sure you're going after them because you want to. Don't make your accomplishments a prerequisite for a relationship. Allow God to coach you every step of the way. When God brings your man on as part of your team, he'll be able to cheer you on and help you accomplish even more goals.

Prayer
God, I thank You that You are showing me every day how great You think I am. I pray that You help me to remember that I am perfect just the way You made me. Whatever goals I have, I pray that they would be rooted in self love and wanting to please You. In Jesus' name, amen!

Journal
What's something you think you need to do before God brings you your man? Write it down and add all the reasons you want to do it. Forget how you think it will make your future man or anyone else feel. How would it make YOU feel to accomplish this goal?

_____

_____

_____

_____

_____

_____

_____

_____

_____

_____

_____

_____

_____

_____

_____

_____

_____

_____

_____

_____

_____

_____

_____

_____

_____

_____

_____

_____

_____

_____

_____

_____

_____

_____

_____

_____

_____

_____

_____

_____

_____

Enjoy Your Freedom

1 Corinthians 7:32-35 NLT

"I want you to be free from the concerns of this life. An unmarried man can spend his time doing the Lord's work and thinking how to please Him. But a married man has to think about his earthly responsibilities and how to please his wife. His interests are divided. In the same way, a woman who is no longer married or has never been married can be devoted to the Lord and holy in body and in spirit. But a married woman has to think about her earthly responsibilities and how to please her husband."

Have you ever been scrolling through social media and seen a cute picture of a couple? Maybe you thought to yourself, "Must be nice. That'll be me one day." Or maybe you're on the other end of the spectrum. You see a picture of a couple and think, "Can y'all get your love off my timeline?" Maybe you go back and forth between these feelings depending on the day. No matter where we fall on the spectrum, it's important that we recognize that there's a level of freedom that comes from being single.

When you get married, "I" and "me" turns to "we" and "us." Want to take a spontaneous trip? Now you have two schedules to work around. Want to move to a different city? Now you have to think about two lives that will be affected by that. Don't get me wrong - it will be nice to have a partner to make decisions with; however, it's important that we don't miss out on the freedom and sovereignty we have right now. God has given us the gift of time to focus on just ourselves and what He's called us to do.

Prayer

God, thank You for the time You've given me to focus on You and have fun. I pray that this time will be something I remember fondly in years to come. I pray that You give me the mindset to fully enjoy my singleness and everything You have for me in this season. In Jesus' name, amen!

Journal

Take a moment and journal about the last thing you did for yourself that didn't require you to think about someone else. Maybe you did something really spontaneous or finally decided to chase a dream you've had for a long time. Consider how great it was to have the freedom of thinking of only yourself in that moment.

_____

_____

_____

_____

_____

_____

_____

_____

_____

_____

Living Single

_____

_____

_____

_____

_____

_____

_____

_____

_____

_____

_____

_____

_____

_____

_____

_____

Devoted to God

1 Corinthians 7:34b-35 GNB

"An unmarried woman or a virgin concerns herself with the Lord's work, because she wants to be dedicated both in body and spirit; but a married woman concerns herself with worldly matters, because she wants to please her husband. I am saying this because I want to help you. I am not trying to put restrictions on you. Instead, I want you to do what is right and proper, and to give yourselves completely to the Lord's service without any reservation."

I want to talk a little more about the freedom that comes with singleness. In our single season, we have complete free rein to devote ourselves fully to God without having to think about anyone else. Now, I don't mean that our pursuits will be selfish. Nine times out of ten, devotion to God requires us to serve Him and His people. We have the luxury of thinking about our purpose and journey for a party of one. However, in marriage, we'll also have to consider if where we feel God leading us is conducive to the lifestyle of our husbands. Even more, we'll eventually have to consider how it will affect our kids.

Right now, we have the chance to devote all of our time and energy in chasing our purpose. Of course when we get married, we'll still be pursuing purpose. In fact - if we follow God correctly - our husbands will add to our purpose journeys. At the same time, we know that our two lives will be made into one, under God's covenant. When this happens, we have to be whole and completely devoted to God. If we're not grounded, we run the risk of losing ourselves in another person or getting caught up in worldly things. I don't know about y'all, but that's not gonna work for me. I'm trying to be fully devoted to God and focused on His purpose for me 24/7. Life is a lot more fun and easier that way!

Prayer
God, I thank You for the opportunity to devote my all to You. Everything I have is Yours. I pray that You would allow me to see more ways where I could be even more engrossed in You. I pray that You continue to reveal my purpose and highest self. I praise You and I thank You, in Jesus' name, amen!

Journal
Journal about some ways you devote yourself to God. Do you spend time with Him? Do you talk to Him and wait for Him to answer? What are some ways you could increase your devotion to God?

_____

_____

_____

_____

_____

_____

_____

_____

_____

_____

_____

Living Single

_____

_____

_____

_____

_____

_____

_____

_____

_____

_____

_____

_____

_____

_____

_____

_____

Being Fruitful

Genesis 1:27-28 NIV
"So God created mankind in his own image, in the image of God he created them; male and female he created them. God blessed them and said to them, "Be fruitful and increase in number; fill the earth and subdue it. Rule over the fish in the sea and the birds in the sky and over every living creature that moves on the ground."

Many of God's instructions throughout the Bible can seem specific to the situations people found themselves in. This is definitely something to consider when reading, but we also have to think deeper about how those stories apply to us today in our current season. There are some experiences and lessons in the Bible that can seem irrelevant to us as singles, but if we take a closer look at them, they can really apply to us where we are now.

Oftentimes when we hear "be fruitful and multiply" we think of this simply as God's instruction to mankind to get married and make babies. While that is true, it can also apply to us in our single season. Bearing fruit and multiplying can look like starting a business, writing a book, encouraging someone, donating to charity, and truly anything that benefits or serves other people. When we do things that show God's character to the world, that's a prime example of us bearing fruit. So, even in your single season it's worth considering - are you being fruitful?

Prayer

God, thank You for creating me to rule over the earth and bear fruit. I pray that You help me to see areas where You have given me authority to plant seeds and watch them grow. I pray that You will continue to build me up into the person You have created me to be. In Jesus' name, amen!

Journal

Take a moment and journal about all the areas in your life where you're being fruitful. Consider if there are any opportunities for you to do more. When you plant seeds and watch them grow, you are walking in the full purpose of who God created you to be!

_____

_____

_____

_____

_____

_____

_____

_____

_____

_____

_____

_____

_____

_____

_____

_____

_____

_____

_____

_____

_____

_____

_____

_____

Forgiveness

Isaiah 61:1-3 NIV
"The Spirit of the Sovereign Lord is on me, because the Lord has anointed me to proclaim good news to the poor. He has sent me to bind up the brokenhearted, to proclaim freedom for the captives and release from darkness for the prisoners, to proclaim the year of the Lord's favor and the day of vengeance of our God, to comfort all who mourn, and provide for those who grieve in Zion— to bestow on them a crown of beauty instead of ashes, the oil of joy instead of mourning, and a garment of praise instead of a spirit of despair. They will be called oaks of righteousness, a planting of the Lord for the display of his splendor."

We all know that wanting to be in a relationship with the man God has for us is going to take some inward work. Part of that work is forgiving people who have hurt us in the past. I don't just mean getting over your ex. I mean really uncovering any scars that are left over from past experiences. For me personally, I have never been in a relationship and I struggled for a long time with feeling undesirable to men. I knew I was pretty, smart, and had all these great qualities, but I assumed guys couldn't see any of that. I came to the realization that if I kept believing that, I would never actually be open to God bringing my husband into my life. I would automatically disqualify myself from what God had for me.

Your trauma and scars may be different than mine. And believe me, we'd be here all day if I wrote about everything I'm working to overcome. I know it's not always a fun process to revisit thoughts or situations that hurt us. However, if we want to truly move on and be ready for God's best, we have to forgive the people and situations that hurt us. Those hurt feelings are taking up space in our hearts that God wants to fill with love. And again, I know it may not be fun or easy, but I promise you God will restore every past hurt, trauma, and situation. Beauty and love is on the other side of your forgiveness.

Prayer

God, I pray that You would be with me as I seek to forgive and move past trauma. I know You have amazing things in store for my future and I let go of the past. I pray that You would continue to soften my heart as I go through the process of forgiving and overcoming. In Jesus' name, amen!

Journal

Write down a past trauma that you struggle to move past. As you reflect on how it has affected you, consider the possible outcomes that overcoming this could have. As you write, remember God loves you and has amazing things in store for you.

_____

_____

_____

_____

_____

_____

_____

_____

_____

_____

Living Single

The Love We Expect

1 Corinthians 13:4-7 NIV
"Love is patient, love is kind. It does not envy, it does not boast, it is not proud. It does not dishonor others, it is not self-seeking, it is not easily angered, it keeps no record of wrongs. Love does not delight in evil but rejoices with the truth. It always protects, always trusts, always hopes, always perseveres."

Have you ever heard that Stephen Chbosky quote, "We accept the love we think we deserve?!" I definitely think this is true. However, I think there's even a way to take that a step further. We expect the love we show to ourselves. That may be confusing, but hear me out. Let's say you take yourself out to eat every Friday night. When you develop a relationship with another person, you'd most likely keep that tradition up. Suddenly your man starts taking you out to eat every Friday night. Not to say you'd set this as an expectation, but it wouldn't shock you if he did this. You'd love it and be open to it. If, by the same token, you're always self-correcting and never applauding yourself for your wins, it could lead to the expectation that your future man should always seek to correct you and never cheer you on.

When we're single, we have the perfect opportunity to set the standard for the love we expect. When we think about love, we should think about it in the context of the way God loves us. He loves with no boundaries, He gives us second chances, He acknowledges how amazing we are - I could go on all day about the way that He loves us. When we think about this love, we should strive to practice it not only in our relationships, but also with ourselves. When we follow His idea of love, our perspective of love will change and we'll be ready to expect the love God has for us.

Prayer

God, I thank You that You are showing me the blueprint for how to love myself. I pray that You would continue to show me how to love myself and others. Through this love, I pray that You would allow me to set a healthy standard for my future relationship. In Jesus' name, amen!

Journal

Write down some ways you practice self-love on a day to day basis. Consider some things you could do or change to align your self-love with the way God loves you.

_____

_____

_____

_____

_____

_____

_____

_____

_____

_____

_____

_____

_____

_____

_____

_____

_____

_____

_____

_____

_____

_____

_____

_____

_____

_____

_____

_____

Be Thankful for the People in Your Life

Ephesians 5:20-21 TPT
"Always give thanks to Father God for every person he brings into your life in the name of our Lord Jesus Christ. And out of your reverence for Christ be supportive of each other in love."

We can't talk about relationships and singleness without talking about cherishing people. There are some people who wait until they have a romantic partner to learn how to cherish and care for someone. That will not be us! Think of all the people you love - your friends, your family, the people you look up to. All of these people are worth being thankful for and cherishing! While we're single, we have the perfect opportunity to grow in how we show our love and appreciation for others. And to be completely honest, navigating a romantic relationship and becoming one with another person seems a lot less intimidating when all your other relationships are beautiful and squared away.

Though we are waiting for God to bring us our husbands, we can be content knowing that He's already brought us people to grow and do life with. In fact, some of the community you have now is going to be vital to the wellbeing and growth of your romantic relationship. When you need someone to check you if you're tripping, your community will hold you accountable. When you want to share a cute thing your man did, your community will be there excited to celebrate with you. I say all of this to stress the importance of cherishing and showing thanks for the people you have now. God put them in your life for a reason.

Prayer

God, I thank You for the amazing people You have brought into my life. Help me to be able to love them and cherish them each and every day. I pray that You would bless them and keep them as we journey through life together. I praise You and I thank You in Jesus' name, amen!

Journal

Take a moment and journal about at least three people you're thankful for. Write down their names and why they're important to you. Then, reach out to them and let them know what you wrote down! Remind them that you cherish them.

_____

_____

_____

_____

_____

_____

_____

_____

_____

_____

_____

_____

_____

_____

_____

_____

_____

_____

_____

_____

_____

_____

_____

_____

_____

_____

Let No One Separate

Matthew 19:4-6 NIV
"Haven't you read," he replied, "that at the beginning the Creator 'made them male and female,' and said, 'For this reason a man will leave his father and mother and be united to his wife, and the two will become one flesh'? So they are no longer two, but one flesh. Therefore what God has joined together, let no one separate."

It is so important to be mindful of who we surround ourselves with. When we're trying to be in a healthy, positive state of mind about relationships, we've got to be careful about who we're talking to and taking advice from. If we're not careful, we can end up allowing other people's opinions and situations to shape our outlook. Though most people mean well, they may not actually be in the position to serve as a positive influence.

When we're moving in a positive direction, we have to make a decision to focus on where God is leading us and people who are on similar journeys. If we partner up and turn to people going in a different direction, we could be led off track. Matthew 19:6b NIV reads, "What God has brought together, let no one separate." This was in direct correlation to a man and woman coming together as one. For our current season, it wouldn't hurt to embrace this idea in a developing sense. Though we can't see it on earth, God has already brought us together with our future husbands. With that in mind, we should commit to the idea of growing with a positive outlook on love and hope for the futures. We can be bonded together as one with this idea and goal of growth. With that bond, should come the ability to not be separated from it no matter what people say or do to us.

Prayer

God, I thank You for the discernment to know who is on the same track as me. I pray that I would only feel led to share and grow with those moving in a positive direction. May no person plant any seeds that would strive to keep me from my future husband. In Jesus' name, amen!

Journal

Take a moment and think about some friends moving in the same direction as you. Write out some ways you all could explore growing together. Maybe you can start a book club, listen to a motivational podcast, or even watch a sermon as a group!

_____

_____

_____

_____

_____

_____

_____

_____

_____

_____

Living Single

_____

_____

_____

_____

_____

_____

_____

_____

_____

_____

_____

_____

_____

_____

_____

_____

What's Your Diet?

Romans 12:2 NIV
"Do not conform to the pattern of this world, but be transformed by the renewing of your mind. Then you will be able to test and approve what God's will is—his good, pleasing and perfect will."

I'm sure you've heard that saying, "You are what you eat." This quote is definitely talking about the food we consume, but it can surely be applied to our overall diet. The shows we watch, the music we listen to, the people we follow on social media - all of it is part of our diet. With that being said, we have to make sure that the content we're feeding ourselves is in line with our goals. For example, if you're trying to break off lust in your life, watching a show that has a lot of sex scenes may not be the move for you. Or let's say, maybe you're feeling really down about being single. Throwing on 90s R&B love songs probably won't help. It may even make you feel a little lonely.

This is to remind you to fix your mind on the higher self you're becoming. When your favorite artist drops a new album, you may not be able to listen to it based on the season of life you're in. Will it be annoying to miss out on the new hit? Honestly, probably. But, what would be even worse is missing out on the life God has for you.

Prayer
Holy Spirit, I pray that you would allow me to discern the things and content I should be taking in. I pray you would allow everything I digest to build me up into a higher version of myself. In Jesus' name, amen!

Journal
Is there anything you should cut out of your diet? Are there things you want to add to your diet? What's something you'd like to consume more of? Consider these questions and write out your answers.

_____

_____

_____

_____

_____

_____

_____

_____

_____

_____

What's Your Dating Budget?

Luke 12:48b NIV
"From everyone who has been given much, much will be demanded; and from the one who has been entrusted with much, much more will be asked."

Have you ever thought about the cost of dating? Whether you're in the dating stage or fully married, you'll be going out to eat and going to experience new things together. All of this can start to add up. I know some of us may be thinking, "Ummm, he's supposed to pay for our dates. That sounds like a problem for him." But let's think beyond money for a second. Have you thought about what dating and being in a relationship will really cost you?

When we get into relationships, there's always a cost associated with it. We may have to pay in the form of vulnerability, transparency, communication, and compromise. When we think about 'cost' in this sense, dating may seem a little pricey. While we're single, it's a good time to consider our dating budget. How vulnerable and transparent are you ready to be? Are you willing to compromise or alter the way you communicate? A certain amount of all of these things will be required in a relationship. Knowing your comfort level now could be helpful in your relationship down the road.

Prayer

God, I pray that You would prepare me to budget for my future relationship now. I believe You are bringing me a man worth the price of getting out of my old ways. I thank You that You are building up me and my future man to be able to have the incredible, anointed relationship that You have for us. In Jesus' name, amen!

Journal

Take a moment and journal about the things you'll have to give up when you get into a relationship. A good way to identify these things could be considering past friendships and romantic relationships. Have you previously had trouble opening up to people? In that case, maybe you could work on using your discernment to be more vulnerable. Do you tend to be stuck in your ways and not want to change? Maybe you could work on your ability to compromise. No matter what you pin point to work on, know that this will not only benefit your future spouse but all of your relationships in the long run.

_____

_____

_____

_____

_____

_____

_____

_____

_____

_____

_____

_____

_____

_____

_____

_____

_____

_____

_____

_____

_____

_____

_____

Find the Time

Matthew 22:36-40 NLT

"Teacher, which is the most important commandment in the law of Moses?" Jesus replied, "'You must love the Lord your God with all your heart, all your soul, and all your mind.' This is the first and greatest commandment. A second is equally important: 'Love your neighbor as yourself.'"

Relationships of any kind take time and energy. Think about your closest friend. Whether you've known this person for a month or ten years, building your relationship took a level of effort. You had to get to know what they like, what they hate, their habits, and the best way they communicate. When God brings you your man, you'll have to go through this process of not only getting to know him, but sharing who you are with him. There will be dates, phone calls, text messages - the whole nine. For some of us, that sounds amazing. We're ready! Where he at? For others of us, this can be an overwhelming thought. We barely have time for a social life now; how are we going to fit in a man?

No matter what end of the spectrum we're on, one thing we need to remember is that the relationship God has for us will require time, attention, and balance. If you have no time in your schedule for a new relationship, it wouldn't be fair for you to commit to a guy right now. He deserves your love and affection! You also have to make some time for a self-care moment. You're a queen. You deserve your own love and affection! And most importantly, you gotta leave some time in there for God. We owe Him our love and affection! I know what you're thinking - that's A LOT of love and affection. Who has the time? We do! God literally created us to love Him, ourselves, and others. It's 100% possible. We just have to find time for it all.

Prayer

God, I thank You that You have created me to love and be loved. Help me to find the time and ways to love those around me and the love You have coming to me. I pray that You would also show me how to love myself and most importantly - You. In Jesus' name, amen!

Journal

Honestly consider if you have time for a romantic relationship right now. If you don't, journal about some ways to make time. If you do, journal about some things you could do during that time to build yourself up and practice extra self care.

_____

_____

_____

_____

_____

_____

_____

_____

_____

_____

Living Single

_____

_____

_____

_____

_____

_____

_____

_____

_____

_____

_____

_____

_____

_____

What Kind of Wife Do You Want to Be?

Proverbs 31:10-12 TPT
"Who could ever find a wife like this one—she is a woman of strength and mighty valor! She's full of wealth and wisdom. The price paid for her was greater than many jewels. Her husband has entrusted his heart to her, for she brings him the rich spoils of victory. All throughout her life she brings him what is good and not evil."

Oftentimes, as women we think about the type of man we want to be with. We think of how he'll treat us, how he'll make us feel, and all the amazing things he'll do for us. Honestly, sometimes it can be fun to think about things like this and talk about it with our girlfriends. But, at the end of the day, God is the one Who knows who our best partner will be. He's in full control.

However, one thing we can control is ourselves. Have you ever thought about the kind of wife you want to be? How do you want to treat your man? How do you want to make him feel? What amazing things do you want to do for him? When it came to Adam and Eve, Eve was created to be a helper for Adam. So just like your man will add great things to your life, you'll add great things to his. You'll be able to love and support him in ways that no one else can. That's so powerful!

Prayer

God, I thank You that You created me to be the perfect helper and more for my future husband. I pray that as we both grow as people, You would show us how to be the best spouses for each other. As I become the woman You created me to be, I know that will fall in line with the wife You've called me to be. I pray for Your full alignment. In Jesus' name, amen!

Journal

Take a moment and write out some of your strongest qualities and/or things that make you a great friend. Consider how these attributes may manifest when you're a wife.

_____

_____

_____

_____

_____

_____

_____

_____

_____

_____

Living Single

_____

_____

_____

_____

_____

_____

_____

_____

_____

_____

_____

_____

_____

_____

_____

_____

_____

_____

_____

_____

_____

_____

_____

_____

_____

_____

_____

_____

_____

_____

_____

_____

_____

_____

Where Did Submission Start?

Genesis 3:16 NLT
"Then he said to the woman, "I will sharpen the pain of your pregnancy, and in pain you will give birth. And you will desire to control your husband, but he will rule over you."

Sooner or later, I think we all knew we were going to cover submission. Before we dive into Scriptures about submission in a marriage, I want to go back to our OGs Adam and Eve. We know that Eve ate the forbidden fruit, Adam followed, and now here we are with sin in the world. Our tendency is to blame Eve. I, however, for a long time thought "Well, Adam didn't play his position. If a man is supposed to lead, then he should have led her away from the fruit." When I explored Genesis more, I found that man and woman were created as mankind and, therefore, equal. It wasn't until Eve ate the forbidden fruit that Adam was set as the leader.

Crazy, right? Because of Sis, now we gotta submit to someone. We can't be too hard on Eve, though. She, like most of us, was an independent woman with her own thoughts and feelings. She just messed up and had to deal with the consequences. Submission started with Eve and it has to start in us, too. This doesn't mean we should submit to just anyone. We should submit to men who mirror God with wisdom, love, and leadership. In mirroring God's wisdom, Adam had been in Eden longer than Eve, giving him better wisdom and understanding of the environment. In showing God's love, we know that Adam loved Eve as his "rib." If the forbidden fruit were to benefit her, he wouldn't have kept it from her. As a reflection of God's leadership, Adam ruled and led animals of all kinds before Eve came into the picture. With these qualities and more, it's fair to say that Adam was worth submitting to. So, as we consider the men God has for us, we have to remember that God is not going to bring us just anyone. He's going to bring us our Adam who is worth submitting to.

Prayer

God, I thank You that You are bringing me a man worth submitting to. I pray that when I'm with him, I see all the qualities that mirror who You are. I pray that You open my heart to the process of submission. In Jesus' name, amen!

Journal

Take a moment and write down any obstacles you may have with submitting. Be honest. Are you strong-willed? Do you like to have things your way? When you're done, write the affirmation "I am capable of submitting to the man God has for me." Repeat this affirmation as much as you need to truly believe it.

_____

_____

_____

_____

_____

_____

_____

_____

_____

_____

Living Single

_____

_____

_____

_____

_____

_____

_____

_____

_____

_____

_____

_____

_____

_____

_____

_____

_____

Submit to Your HUSBAND

Ephesians 5:22-24 NIV
"Wives, submit yourselves to your own husbands as you do to the Lord. For the husband is the head of the wife as Christ is the head of the church, his body, of which he is the Savior. Now as the church submits to Christ, so also wives should submit to their husbands in everything."

So, let's talk about submission a little more. Biblically, we are told to submit to our husbands as the church submits to Jesus. For a lot of us, myself included, this instruction feels like a lot. Honestly, the thing that gives me comfort here is the key word 'HUSBAND.' The Bible does not say submit to your boyfriend or even your fiancé. To me, submission is the beginning of what I like to think of as 'The Husband Package.'

'The Husband Package' comes with great perks such as living together, building a family, having sex, and submission on our part. Depending on your preference, this package could be a little different and even include cooking, cleaning, and things of that nature. Perks that are a part of 'The Husband Package' require an investment of a proposal and wedding vows. Prior to this inquiry to invest in a higher package, there are pre-packages. These pre-packages can give you experiences that show you if your man is eligible for an upgrade. With the boyfriend/fiancé package, you should be able to see Christ Like leadership qualities in your man. These attributes can give you glimpses that submission wouldn't be so bad to a qualified man. When those moments pop up, take notice and stay open-minded!

Prayer

God, I pray that You soften my heart and make me more open to the concept of submitting to my husband. As You lead me through life, I pray that You would highlight a man to me that is worthy of this and only has my best interests at heart. I praise You and I thank You that all these things are already done in Jesus' name, amen!

Journal

Take a moment and journal about some qualities that would make you want to submit to a man.

_____

_____

_____

_____

_____

_____

_____

_____

_____

_____

_____

Living Single

So, What Are We?

James 1:19 NIV
"My dear brothers and sisters, take note of this: Everyone should be quick to listen, slow to speak and slow to become angry."

At some point in a relationship the question "What are we?" or "What are we doing?" is going to come up. Honestly, it would be great and super ideal if this wasn't the case. If we could all read each other's minds and be on the same page, that would be dope. But since that isn't possible, we HAVE to openly and honestly communicate.

Communicating and setting clear boundaries is vital in any relationship. It saves everyone from pain and heartache later down the road. Having a high level of communication and transparency from the beginning of a relationship can also help set the standard for the road ahead. Even if you stay on the same page about the status of your relationship, there will still be plenty of other opportunities to communicate differing opinions and even have tough conversations. When a relationship is built on the foundation of good communication, it can only flourish and grow from there. Whether there's marriage at the end of the journey or not, there will definitely be some feelings and pain saved by being open and honest.

Prayer
God, I thank You that You have given me the proper speech and tools to address and communicate my feelings. I pray that as I enter into romantic and even friendly relations, that You would allow me to use those tools. In Jesus' name, amen!

Journal
Take a moment and write out some ways you could grow into a better communicator. Do you listen to respond or listen to understand? Are you easily offended when no one meant any harm to you? In general, what are some areas you could develop your communication?

_____

_____

_____

_____

_____

_____

_____

_____

_____

_____

_____

Living Single

Waiting for Cake

Hebrews 13:4 NIV
"Marriage should be honored by all, and the marriage bed kept pure, for God will judge the adulterer and all the sexually immoral."

Have you ever licked the bowl while baking the cake? It's honestly delicious. But could you imagine eating an entire cake's worth of cake batter? Not only would you get tired of it, but you'd also probably get sick. This is what we look like having sex before we get married. Hear me out.

Think about it this way. Let's say your relationship with your future husband is like a cake. Before you can even start the process, you need the ingredients. This is like the process of us becoming whole individuals while we're single. Then, it's time to start mixing the batter. Your ingredients mix with your husband's ingredients, and the batter is starting to come together nicely! Now let's say you decide that instead of putting the batter in the oven of marriage, you just start eating the batter. At this point you're looking at a stomach ache or some kind of sickness. This is the same with sex. If we indulge too soon we run the risk of hurt feelings, life long connections that should not be formed, and worst of all STDs. So eating the batter may be good to us at the moment, but in the end a fully baked cake that requires us to wait is better for us.

Prayer

God, I pray that You give me the tools and the patience to wait to have sex. Build up my endurance and resilience in You so that I may experience the fullness of how You intended for sex to be. In Jesus' name I pray, amen!

Journal

Are you waiting to have sex? If you are, journal about why. Try to think of deeper, personal reasons outside of just following scripture. If you're not waiting, journal about why not. Consider for yourself if the good outweighs the possible negative outcomes. No matter what you're journaling about for this prompt, remember to take your choices to God. Have a conversation with Him about your decisions and why you've landed where you are.

_____

_____

_____

_____

_____

_____

_____

_____

_____

Living Single

_____

_____

_____

_____

_____

_____

_____

_____

_____

_____

_____

_____

_____

_____

_____

_____

Love is More Than Sex

1 Corinthians 6:18 NIV
"Flee from sexual immorality. All other sins a person commits are outside the body, but whoever sins sexually, sins against their own body."

For a large portion of my life, my idea of love centered around sex in a major way. Whenever I thought about marriage, my next thought would be sex. Whenever I would try to gauge if a man found me attractive, I'd wonder "Does he want to have sex with me?" This obviously isn't healthy. There is so much more to a relationship than sex. Should our future husbands find us attractive? 100%, yes. However, wanting to get in bed with us should never be the driving force of the attraction.

When we read the Bible, there are so many Scriptures that teach us to stay away from sexual immorality. This includes sex before marriage. However, there aren't any passages that truly warn against loving someone from a place of pure intentions. When we're in the process of coming together with our men, we need to come with a mindset of purity. Our intentions, thoughts, and actions should all reflect purity and seeking genuine human connection. If thoughts of lust rise up, which they probably will because we're only human, we have to have a plan in place to keep them at bay.

Prayer
God, I thank You that You created me with a pure heart and a pure mind. I block out any distractions that may try to take my focus from that. I pray that You would continue to give me the strength, power, and tools to stay in line with Your thoughts. In Jesus' name, amen!

Journal
Take a moment and journal about some emotionally intimate actions or activities you could do with your future husband that exclude physical intimacy.

_____

_____

_____

_____

_____

_____

_____

_____

_____

_____

Living Single

What Are Your Physical Boundaries?

James 1:13-15 NIV
"When tempted, no one should say, "God is tempting me." For God cannot be tempted by evil, nor does He tempt anyone; but each person is tempted when they are dragged away by their own evil desire and enticed. Then, after desire has conceived, it gives birth to sin; and sin, when it is full-grown, gives birth to death."

Alright, so I'm gonna be super transparent with you all. I have often thought about how far is too far when it comes to physical intimacy. Obviously when we're married, the marriage bed is undefiled. We'll be able to have all the fun with our husbands. However, when you're dating and engaged, how much fun do you want to have? Like, is kissing okay? How about a booty grab? What about sleeping in the same bed? Where is your boundary for physical intimacy?

This is important to consider now because dating is an evaluation process. You're learning about a new person, opening up, and figuring out if your relationship can go the distance. Without physical boundaries, this process runs the risk of being impeded by lust or sexual immorality. Physical intimacy is super powerful. I know for me personally, if I'm in bed with my future man, it could be a short trip to crossing a line. Because I know that about myself, I know that - though it would be fun - napping or sleeping in bed with my man before marriage would be hard to handle. Your boundaries may be different. Maybe you're fine with sharing a bed but certain physical acts would feel like a gateway activity to crossing the line. Whatever your boundaries are, it's important to have them in mind as you enter a relationship. This way, you can be clear with your man and stay focused on developing your relationship.

Prayer

God, I pray that You would help me to set healthy physical boundaries. I pray that You would show me where my temptation lies and how to avoid falling for them. I thank You that You have given me the power to be patient and strong willed. In Jesus' name, amen!

Journal

Take some time and journal about the physical boundaries you'd like to set. What are some things that are tempting for you? What are some gateway activities that could lead to crossing the line? Be honest with yourself! And remember, the boundary you set while dating can be lifted when you're married.

_____

_____

_____

_____

_____

_____

_____

_____

_____

_____

Living Single

_____

_____

_____

_____

_____

_____

_____

_____

_____

_____

_____

_____

_____

_____

_____

_____

Praying Against Counterfeits in Your Life

Matthew 7:17-20 NLT
"A good tree produces good fruit, and a bad tree produces bad fruit. A good tree can't produce bad fruit, and a bad tree can't produce good fruit. So every tree that does not produce good fruit is chopped down and thrown into the fire. Yes, just as you can identify a tree by its fruit, so you can identify people by their actions."

Sis, the man God has for you is out there. He's fine. He's caring. He's going to be a great leader of your future household, among other amazing things. Though I know this, I don't know exactly how God is going to bring him to you. Some of us may have to kiss a few frogs and date around. Some of us may be told exactly who our husband is. God is capable of doing literally anything, so there's no real telling how it will happen.

One thing we can be sure of though, is that while God is bringing us the men He has for us, the enemy will try to put men in front of us who seem like the one. But because the enemy isn't that slick, the counterfeit guys he brings us will probably have something off about them. For example, you could meet a man who's fine and really nice, but he doesn't believe in God. You might start thinking, "Oh, well I can just take him to church with me or bring him to my Bible study." That's a great option as a friend! However, when God brings us our husband and it's time for us to be together, He's not going to bring us a fixer upper. He's going to bring us someone on our level who we can grow and mature with. It should never be up to us to "fix" someone. It's always up to God to make someone whole. If he's not whole and you're not whole, he's not the one and/or it's not the time to get together yet.

Prayer

God, I pray for Your discernment as I go through life in anticipation and preparation for my future marriage. I pray that You would allow me to see the man You have for me through Your eyes and in Your timing. Any distractions that come my way will have no effect on me as I walk in alignment with Your plan. In Jesus' name, amen!

Journal

Write a letter to your future self to congratulate her on marrying her man. Celebrate with her! Applaud her for overcoming and being patient. She did that!

_____

_____

_____

_____

_____

_____

_____

_____

_____

_____

Living Single

Naked and Unashamed

Genesis 2:25; 3:6-7 NLT

"Now the man and his wife were both naked, but they felt no shame. ---- The woman was convinced. She saw that the tree was beautiful and its fruit looked delicious, and she wanted the wisdom it would give her. So she took some of the fruit and ate it. Then she gave some to her husband, who was with her, and he ate it, too. At that moment their eyes were opened, and they suddenly felt shame at their nakedness. So they sewed fig leaves together to cover themselves."

When Adam and Eve were in Eden, they were completely naked and unashamed. When we read this, we know it's speaking to them being physically naked. Being naked before someone can be a sign of comfort and vulnerability. Adam and Eve were vulnerable not only physically, but emotionally and spiritually too. They shared a perfect garden and lived every day in paradise. However, when Eve was vulnerable with the wrong being, it led her down the wrong path and straight to the forbidden fruit.

Looking at the first God-ordained human relationship, we see that being naked and unashamed with our life partner is the basis of how we should be. When we open ourselves to the wrong influence, that's when things start to go off course. When God brings us the right man, we know we'll be able to be honest and vulnerable with him. The hard part is that we may have past experiences with the wrong influences that have built us up to be guarded. We have every right to protect ourselves. God doesn't want us out here willy nilly giving our hearts and transparency to just anyone. At the same time, we have to remember that when God brings the right man into our lives, we are predestined to be vulnerable and comfortable with him. We'll be comfortable enough to be completely naked and unashamed.

Prayer

God, I thank You for Your wisdom and discernment. I pray that when You bring the right man to me, I'll be able to be completely honest and vulnerable with him. I won't hold him accountable for the mistakes of people before him. I will see him the way You intend for me to see him, as my life partner who I can share my heart with. In Jesus' name, amen!

Journal

Take a moment and journal about some valuable qualities in a person that make you feel like you can be vulnerable with them. Consider things like how you communicate best and the traits of a good partner. While journaling, be sure to check in with God along the way to make sure you're on the same page with your vision of a relationship.

_____

_____

_____

_____

_____

_____

_____

_____

_____

Living Single

_____

_____

_____

_____

_____

_____

_____

_____

_____

_____

_____

_____

_____

_____

_____

_____

_____

Pray for Your Future Husband

Philippians 4:6-7 NIV
"Do not be anxious about anything, but in every situation, by prayer and petition, with thanksgiving, present your requests to God. And the peace of God, which transcends all understanding, will guard your hearts and your minds in Christ Jesus."

Even though it may seem weird and uncomfortable, it's okay - and even encouraged - to pray for your future husband. I can't hold you, it sounded weird to me at first. I used to think, "How am I supposed to pray for someone I don't know? Also, what if he's not praying for me? I'm not about to be out here thinking about someone who's not thinking about me." Now, the present version of me would respond with, "You don't know him, but God does. Also, you have no real idea if he's praying for you. What do you have to lose by speaking life over him?" So all the things I said to my past-self, I'm about to reiterate to you.

Pray for your future husband. My guess is that if you're reading this devotional, you've either already done this or you've heard of the concept and haven't tried it yet. If you've already done it, it doesn't hurt to do it again! If you haven't done it yet, here's a great chance to start! Think about it, at some point this man is going to be the leader of your household and the two of you will be together forever. Why not start protecting him and praying for him now? You never know. The prayer you pray today could be the prayer that makes things better when you marry your man. Praying now could cut down your worrying later.

Prayer

God, I thank You for the man You have called to be my husband. I pray that You would be with him all the days of his life. If he has any need for prayer, I pray that You would put it on my heart to pray for him. I thank You for the man he is and the man he is becoming. In Jesus' name, amen!

Journal

Write down some things you're struggling with in life right now. You can be as general or specific as you would like. When you're done, pray that you would be free from and overcome these struggles. After that, cover those same issues in prayer for your husband.

_____

_____

_____

_____

_____

_____

_____

_____

_____

_____

_____

_____

_____

_____

_____

_____

_____

_____

_____

_____

_____

_____

_____

_____

Praying Against Counterfeits in Your Husband's Life

Mark 10: 6-8 NIV
"But at the beginning of creation God 'made them male and female.' 'For this reason a man will leave his father and mother and be united to his wife, and the two will become one flesh.' So they are no longer two, but one flesh."

I cannot stress this enough - you are somebody's wife. Your man is somewhere out here working on himself and will be looking for his wife when the time is right. Knowing that, we have to know that the enemy may try to present your man with a detour on the way to you. We're not about to have that, so we're going to pray against it.

This prayer protects your husband from distractions, new soul ties, and hurt feelings. God is currently working on you and your future husband separately for a reason. While God's working on both of you, placing the focus on Him and His work is important. Less distractions for your man means more time and focus on God developing him. Praying against counterfeits also sets up protection for your man's heart. Your prayers could help your husband avoid a toxic or heartbreaking situation on his way to you.

Prayer

God, thank You for the husband You're going to bring into my life. I pray that You would guard his heart and mind, allowing him to focus on You. I pray against any distractions or counterfeits that may come his way. I pray that You would reveal these counterfeits to him for what they are and allow him to stay on the course that You have set out for him. In Jesus' name I pray, amen!

Journal

As you're growing and developing through ups and downs, so is your man. Take a moment and write an encouraging letter to your future husband. Give him the encouragement to keep going!

_____

_____

_____

_____

_____

_____

_____

_____

_____

Living Single

_____

_____

_____

_____

_____

_____

_____

_____

_____

_____

_____

_____

_____

_____

_____

_____

He Wants to Be Married

Genesis 2:23-25 GNB
*"Then the man said, 'At last, here is one of my own kind—
Bone taken from my bone, and flesh from my flesh. "Woman"
is her name because she was taken out of man.' That is why a
man leaves his father and mother and is united with his wife,
and they become one."*

Though it may not seem like it in society right now, God
created men to desire companionship and a wife. When God
created Adam, one of the first things He said was "It is not
good for the man to live alone. I will make a suitable
companion to help him." (Genesis 2:18 GNB) God created
animals of all kinds and none of them were suitable partners
for Adam. That's when He put Adam in a deep sleep, took a
rib from him, and created Eve. God had full capability to create
Eve from dust, but instead He took a part of Adam to create
her. When Adam woke up, he was excited to find Eve as a
suitable partner that came from his flesh.

This truly shows us that men and women were literally created
for each other. Now, we have many more distractions and
complications than Adam and Eve had at the time. This story
is even pre-forbidden fruit consumption. But even with all our
distractions, we have to remember our roots and who God
created us to be. If you and your man are in alignment with
God, in His timing, your husband will realize you're a breath of
fresh air. You're THE suitable partner he's always been
searching for.

Prayer

God, I thank You that You have created me and my man as suitable partners. I pray that You would help us get past any distractions and get us back to the root of who we are not only as humans, but as individuals. In Jesus' name, amen!

Journal

Write yourself an affirming reminder letter that your man wants to be married. Between casual dating and everything we see in society, this can definitely be hard to believe so you might need a reminder every now and then. Check back in with this note whenever you need a reminder of what it says!

_____

_____

_____

_____

_____

_____

_____

_____

_____

Living Single

_____

_____

_____

_____

_____

_____

_____

_____

_____

_____

_____

_____

_____

_____

_____

_____

Your Man Should Practice Self Love

Ephesians 5:28 NIV
"In this same way, husbands ought to love their wives as their own bodies. He who loves his wife loves himself."

When we think of self-care and self-love, we often think of women and femininity. This is the most baffling thing, if you think about it, because everyone should practice self-love. We've discussed it a few times in this journey, but when someone loves themselves, it makes them better equipped to love others and be loved. This doesn't just apply to us as women. This is also a standard we should hold our future husbands to.

Biblically, we are all instructed to love our neighbors as ourselves, which all starts with self-love. However, in Ephesians 5:28 men specifically are required to "love their wives as their own bodies". This passage basically tells us that a man is to care for his wife in the same way he cares for himself. With that in mind, if a man doesn't endorse some kind of self-love or self-care, it may be hard for him to love and care about the woman he's with. So when you're in the space of dating and being pursued by a man, check in on his level of self-care. Does he work out? Does he eat healthy? What's his self-confidence looking like? All these things will give you hints on his capacity to love a woman.

Prayer
God, I thank You that the man You're bringing into my life loves himself. I thank You that he is fully aware of the love that You have for him. I pray that You would continue to empower him and show him the healthiest way to love himself. In Jesus' name, amen!

Journal
Take a moment and write down some ways a man can practice self care. Let this list open your mind to the ways men take care of themselves so that when you're looking for it, you can see some signs of it.

_____

_____

_____

_____

_____

_____

_____

_____

_____

_____

His Love Should Mirror God's Love

Ephesians 5:25-27 NIV
"Husbands, love your wives, just as Christ loved the church and gave himself up for her to make her holy, cleansing her by the washing with water through the word, and to present her to himself as a radiant church, without stain or wrinkle or any other blemish, but holy and blameless."

Have you ever really considered how much Jesus loves us? He took on every one of our sins and died for things he wasn't even guilty of. Died a full death. For us. That's a crazy amount of care for another being. The craziest thing about all of this is that we didn't have to do anything to earn this love AND it's completely unconditional. No matter what we do, Jesus will always be our Big Brother interceding to our Father in Heaven on our behalf. The thing that continues to blow my mind is that God is bringing us a man that will emulate the love that Jesus has for us.

Now, notice I said emulate. No person could ever love us to the exact degree that Jesus loves us. It's actually, literally impossible. However, our spouse will be called and ordained to love us the way Jesus loves us. Our future husbands will always speak positive words over us and treat us with the utmost respect, emotionally and physically. I want us to remember this, because as we are pursued by a man, these are the types of qualities we should be on the lookout for. I'm not saying that on the first date the man should be in love with you. However, he should be speaking highly of you and treating you with respect. At the end of the day, the man God has for you is going to be an extension of His love. If nothing about a guy says that, it's a clear indication that he's not the one.

Prayer

God, I thank You that You are bringing me a man whose love will mirror the love that You have for me. I pray that You will allow me to spot the qualities that signal to me a man who's following in Your footsteps. I thank You for the never ending love You have for me. I receive it right now in Jesus' name, amen!

Journal

Write out some examples of Jesus' love for you. It could be the fact that you woke up this morning or even the fact that Jesus died on the cross for your sins. Now take a moment to rest in and feel what it's like to be loved by Him.

Living Single

You Have Everything You Need

Romans 8:28-30 NLT

"And we know that God causes everything to work together for the good of those who love God and are called according to his purpose for them. For God knew his people in advance, and he chose them to become like his Son, so that his Son would be the firstborn among many brothers and sisters. And having chosen them, he called them to come to him. And having called them, he gave them right standing with himself. And having given them right standing, he gave them his glory."

No matter what you take away from reading and engaging with this book, I truly pray that you recognize that you are whole and complete, lacking nothing. When God created you, he had a full and complete idea for who you are and why you are needed for such a time as this. Your purpose doesn't start when you get in a relationship. Right now you have every single thing you need inside of you. You're smart. You're beautiful. You're passionate. You're driven.

Even as you read this, I may not know you personally but I know the God who created you. He has beautiful things in store for you. You can't even begin to imagine what He wants to show you. I truly pray that while you're in your season of singleness, you get to know yourself and God on the deepest possible level. If you only knew the things you can accomplish with a full understanding of who you are, it would blow your mind! So as you go through your journey of singleness and eventually into marriage, always remember who you are. You are a daughter of God! He created you in His image.

Prayer

God, I thank You that You have created me to be whole and complete. I pray that You would continue to show me reminders everyday of who I am and who You created me to be. In Jesus' name, amen!

Journal

Take a moment and journal about what being a daughter of God means to you.

_____

_____

_____

_____

_____

_____

_____

_____

_____

_____

_____

Living Single

Bible Translations

TPT - The Passion Translation
NLT - New Living Translation
NKJV - New King James Version
GNB - Good News Bible, also known as the Good News
Translation
NIV - New International Version

Made in the USA
Middletown, DE
08 March 2022

62340304R00075